PRESENTED TO

BY

ON

Read *With* Me — Bible Series

Wise Words of the Bible

Illustrated by
Dennis Jones

Edited by
Catherine DeVries

ZondervanPublishingHouse

Grand Rapids, Michigan

Contents

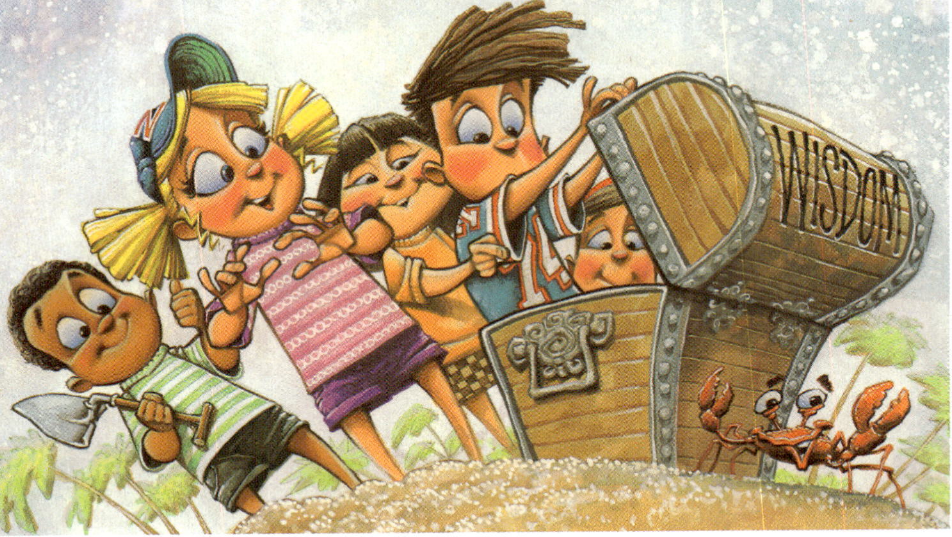
WISDOM

Good Thoughts

Philippians 4:8

Always think about what is true. Think about what is noble, right and pure. Think about what is lovely and worthy of respect. If anything is excellent or worthy of praise, think about those kinds of things.

Being Honest

Leviticus 19:11

Do not tell lies.

1 Chronicles 29:17

My God, I know that you put our hearts to the test. And you are pleased when we are honest.

Zechariah 8:16

Here is what you must do. Speak the truth to one another.

Being Gentle

Ezekiel 34:16

I will bandage the ones that are hurt. I will make the weak ones stronger.

Philippians 4:5

Let everyone know how gentle you are.

1 Thessalonians 2:7

But we were gentle among you. We were like a mother caring for her little children.

Trusting in God

Psalm 62:8

Trust in God at all times, you people. Tell him all of your troubles. God is our place of safety.

Proverbs 3:5–6

Trust in the LORD with all your heart. Do not depend on your own understanding. In all your ways remember him. Then he will make your paths smooth and straight.

Friends

Proverbs 16:28
Those who talk about others come between close friends.

Proverbs 17:17
Friends love at all times. They are there to help when trouble comes.

Proverbs 27:10
Don't desert your friends.

Keep on Going

1 Corinthians 9:24

In a race all the runners run. But only one gets the prize. You know that, don't you? So run in a way that will get you the prize.

Hebrews 12:1–2

Let us throw off any sin that holds on to us so tightly. Let us keep on running the race marked out for us. Let us keep looking to Jesus.

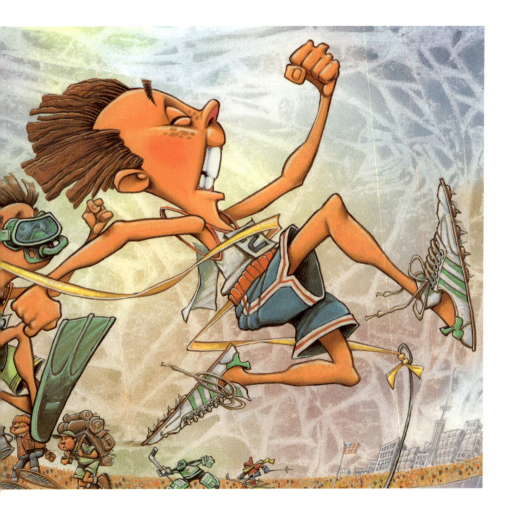

When You Are Tempted

1 Corinthians 10:13

God is faithful. He will not let you be tempted any more than you can take. But when you are tempted, God will give you a way out so that you can stand up under it.

Hebrews 2:18

Jesus himself suffered when he was tempted. Now he is able to help others who are being tempted.

20

What Makes You Beautiful?

1 Peter 3:3–4

Braiding your hair doesn't make you beautiful. Wearing gold jewelry or fine clothes doesn't make you beautiful. Instead, your beauty comes from inside you. It is the beauty of a gentle and quiet spirit. Beauty like that doesn't fade away. God places great value on it.

When You Are Tired

Isaiah 40:29–31

The LORD God gives strength to those who are tired. He gives power to those who are weak. Even young people become worn out and get tired. But those who trust in the LORD will receive new strength. They will fly as high as eagles.

Don't Compare

Romans 7:7

Do not want what belongs to other people.

Galatians 6:4

Each person should put his own actions to the test. He shouldn't compare himself to someone else. Each of you should carry your own load.

1 Timothy 6:6

You must be happy with what you have.

Giving

Proverbs 21:26

Godly people give without holding back.

Matthew 10:8

Give freely.

Acts 20:35

It is more blessed to give than to receive.

Love

1 Corinthians 13:4, 6–8

Love is patient. Love is kind. It is full of joy when the truth is spoken. It always protects. It always trusts. It always hopes. It never gives up. Love never fails.

1 Peter 4:8

Love one another deeply. Love erases many sins by forgiving them.

Sticking to Your Faith

Ephesians 6:11, 14–17

Put on all of God's armor. Then you can stand firm against the devil's evil plans. Put the belt of truth around your waist. Put the armor of godliness on your chest. Wear on your feet what will prepare you to tell the good news of peace. Also, pick up the shield of faith. With it you can put out all of the flaming arrows of the evil one. Put on the helmet of salvation. And take the sword of the Holy Spirit. The sword is God's word.

Being Kind
to People in Need

Proverbs 14:31

Anyone who is kind to those in need honors God.

Proverbs 16:24

Pleasant words are like honey. They are sweet to the spirit and bring healing to the body.

Romans 12:13

Share with God's people who are in need.

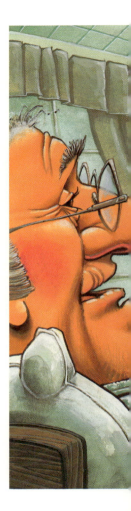

No Pride

Ephesians 4:2

Don't be proud at all. Be completely gentle. Be patient. Put up with one another in love.

1 Peter 5:5

All of you, put on a spirit that is free of pride toward each other as if it were your clothes.

Anger

Philippians 2:14

Do everything without finding fault or arguing.

James 1:19–20

Everyone should be quick to listen. But they should be slow to speak. They should be slow to get angry. Anger doesn't produce the kind of life God wants.

Taking Care of Animals

Genesis 1:26

Then God said, "Let us make man in our likeness. Let them rule over the fish in the waters and the birds of the air. Let them rule over the livestock and over the whole earth."

Proverbs 12:10

Those who do what is right take good care of their animals.

A Happy Heart

Proverbs 15:13

A happy heart makes a face look cheerful.

Proverbs 17:22

A cheerful heart makes you healthy.

Getting Along

Joshua 24:15

As for me and my family, we will serve the LORD.

Proverbs 3:33

The LORD blesses the homes of those who do what is right.

Romans 12:18

If possible, live in peace with everyone. Do that as much as you can.

2 Corinthians 13:11

Agree with one another. Live in peace.

When You Worry

Psalm 55:22

Turn your worries over to the LORD. He will keep you going.

Psalm 56:3–4

When I'm afraid, I will trust in you. I trust in God. I praise his word. I trust in God. I will not be afraid.

Wisdom

Proverbs 2:2, 4

Let your ears listen to wisdom. Apply your heart to understanding. Look for it as you would look for silver. Search for it as you would search for hidden treasure.

James 3:17

The wisdom that comes from heaven is pure. That's the most important thing about it. It also loves peace. It thinks about others. It obeys. It is full of mercy and good fruit. It is fair. It doesn't pretend to be what it is not.

God's Beautiful World

Psalm 104:24–26, 31

LORD, you have made so many things! How wise you were when you made all of them! The earth is full of your creatures. Look at the ocean, so big and wide! It is filled with more creatures than people can count. It is filled with living things, from the largest to the smallest. Ships sail back and forth on it. May the glory of the LORD continue forever. May the LORD be happy with what he has made.

When You Are Sad

Psalm 42:5

My spirit, why are you so sad? Why are you so upset deep down inside me? Put your hope in God.

Luke 6:21

Blessed are you who are sad now. You will laugh.

2 Corinthians 7:6

God comforts those who are sad.

Working Hard

Colossians 3:23–24

Work at everything you do with all your heart. Work because you know that you will finally receive as a reward what the Lord wants you to have. You are serving the Lord Christ.

Being Selfish

Proverbs 3:28

Suppose you have something to give. Don't say to your neighbor, "Come back later. I'll give it to you tomorrow."

Matthew 5:42

Give to the one who asks you for something. Don't turn away from the one who wants to borrow something from you.

Philippians 2:3

Don't do anything only to get ahead. Don't do it because you are proud. Instead, be free of pride. Think of others as better than yourselves.

Praising God

Psalm 13:6

I will sing to the LORD. He has been so good to me.

Psalm 147:1

How good it is to sing praises to our God!

Psalm 149:1

Praise the LORD. Sing a new song to the LORD. Sing praise to him in the community of his faithful people.

Doing What
Mom and Dad Say

Ephesians 6:1

Children, obey your parents as
believers in the Lord. Obey them
because it's the right thing to do.

Colossians 3:20

Obey your parents in everything.
That pleases the Lord.

Praying

Matthew 6:6

When you pray, go into your room. Close the door and pray to your Father [in heaven].

Ephesians 6:18

At all times, pray by the power of the Spirit. Pray all kinds of prayers. Always keep on praying for all of God's people.

Philippians 4:6

Don't worry about anything. Instead, tell God about everything. Ask and pray. Give thanks to him.

1 Thessalonians 5:17

Never stop praying.

Project Management and Editorial: **Catherine DeVries**
Interior Art and Cover Art: **Dennis Jones**
Interior Design: **Sue Vandenberg Koppenol**
Cover Design: **Jody Langley**
Printing: **Quebecor Printing, Kingsport, TN**